Leonardo da Vinci
1452-1519

Leonardo da Vinci (1452-1519) was born in Italy, the son of a gentleman of Florence. He made significant contributions to many different disciplines, including anatomy, botany, geology, astronomy, architecture, paleontology, and cartography.

He is one of the greatest and most influential painters of all time, creating masterpieces such as the *Mona Lisa* and *The Last Supper*. And his imagination led him to create designs for things such as an armored car, scuba gear, a parachute, a revolving bridge, and flying machines. Many of these ideas were so far ahead of their time that they weren't built until centuries later.

He is the original "Renaissance Man" whose genius extended to all five areas of today's STEAM curriculum: Science, Technology, Engineering, the Arts, and Mathematics.

You can find more information on Leonardo da Vinci in *Who Was Leonardo da Vinci?* by Roberta Edwards (Grosset & Dunlap, 2005), *Magic Tree House Fact Tracker: Leonardo da Vinci* by Mary Pope Osborne and Natalie Pope Bryce (Random House, 2009), and *Leonardo da Vinci for Kids: His Life and Ideas* by Janis Herbert (Chicago Review Press, 1998).

LITTLE LEONARDO'S™

Fascinating World of MATH

Illustrated by
GREG PAPROCKI

Written by
BOB COOPER

$E = mc^2$

$(a+b)^2 = a^2 + 2ab + b^2$

$v = \frac{s}{t}$

$(a-b)(a-b) = a^2 + b^2$

f

x

$hx = 8 - 3y^2$

sin

$3 \times 9 =$

$x^2 + 3x$ $2 \times 2 = 4$

GIBBS SMITH
TO ENRICH AND INSPIRE HUMANKIND

MATHEMATICS provides the basic building blocks for science, engineering, technology, and some of the arts.

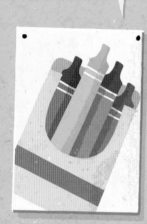

Understanding math begins with our NUMBER SYSTEM.
We use a DECIMAL system, which means it
includes ten different NUMERALS: 0, 1, 2, 3, 4, 5, 6, 7, 8, and 9.

0

1

The simplest use of numbers is to COUNT how much there is of
something. The numeral 0 (ZERO) means there's nothing. The other
numerals, from 1 to 9, represent increasingly larger amounts.

2

3

4   5

By combining these we can make numbers larger
than 9—starting with 10, 11, and 12 . . . and *much* larger numbers
like 50, 100, 762, 91,854, or 3,659,012,877.

. . . 48, 49, 50 . . .

Numbers are also used to MEASURE size or amount. We use rulers and tape measures to measure LENGTH. Scales measure weight. Watches and clocks measure time. Thermometers are used to measure temperature.

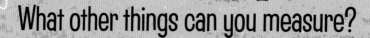

What other things can you measure?

A football field includes measurements right on the field. There are hash marks 1 yard apart, and the number of yards from the 50-yard line to each goal line is marked every 10 yards.

Understanding numbers and what they
are used for helps us understand our world.

ARITHMETIC is one thing we do with numbers
every day. The basic operations of arithmetic are
addition, subtraction, multiplication, and division.

Helping with grocery shopping, you can use ADDITION to add the prices of items to make sure you have enough money for everything.

You helped plan the family road trip to the Grand Canyon.
The map showed that it's 450 miles away.

After driving more than 5 hours, you use SUBTRACTION to find that you
still have to go 450 miles minus the 375 miles shown on the car's
odometer that you've already traveled, which equals 75 miles.

If a recipe serves a certain number of people but you're cooking for a different number, you can use multiplication and division to figure out the proper amount of ingredients.

You're helping make some omelets. The recipe says to use 3 eggs for 1 omelet, and you're making 4 omelets. You **MULTIPLY 3 eggs** times **4 omelets** to find that you'll need **12 eggs**.

You chop up 8 tablespoons of fresh parsley. **DIVIDE 8 tablespoons** by **4 omelets** to find that you can sprinkle **2 tablespoons** on each omelet.

We use FRACTIONS to count *part* of something—an amount that's *more* than nothing (0) but *less* than one whole thing (1). If you're really hungry and eat 3 of the 8 pieces of pizza, the fraction $\frac{3}{8}$ shows how much of the pizza you ate.

Numbers mentioned so far have been zero and numbers *more than zero*. Numbers that are more than zero are called POSITIVE NUMBERS.

Positive numbers are like riding up in an elevator from the ground floor of a building to the upper floors. As you go up, the floor numbers increase: 1, 2, 3, and so on.

If the building also has underground levels, you can ride the elevator down past the ground floor. Think of these numbers as NEGATIVE NUMBERS (*less than zero*). We write these as –1, –2, and say "minus one" and "minus two."

3

2

1

B1

B2

B3

A cool way to think about all the numbers we've seen so far is to look at them on a NUMBER LINE.

If we flip the building on its side, we can think of ground level as the number 0. The main floors of the building are positive numbers and go to the right of 0. The underground levels are negative numbers and go to the left of 0.

-3   -2   -1   0

← NEGATIVE NUMBERS

We can even put our $\frac{3}{8}$ fraction on the number line. It goes between 0 and 1, since we know it's more than 0 and less than 1.

POSITIVE NUMBERS ⟶

A number line is a way to look at a group of numbers as a picture. It's a basic GRAPH. Graphs can use lines, shapes, and even colors to make numbers easier to understand.

Graphs are good for showing how things change over time, like the weather. You could use a thermometer to measure and write down the temperature every hour during the day.

Time	Temperature
7 a.m.	62°
8 a.m.	63°
9 a.m.	64°
10 a.m.	66°
11 a.m.	68°
12 p.m.	71°
1 p.m.	73°
2 p.m.	75°
3 p.m.	76°
4 p.m.	77°
5 p.m.	80°
6 p.m.	78°
7 p.m.	77°
8 p.m.	74°
9 p.m.	71°

A list of numbers doesn't tell as good a story as a graph.

We can create a simple graph by putting two different number lines together: one that shows the TIME of day going from left to right, and one that shows the TEMPERATURE going up and down.

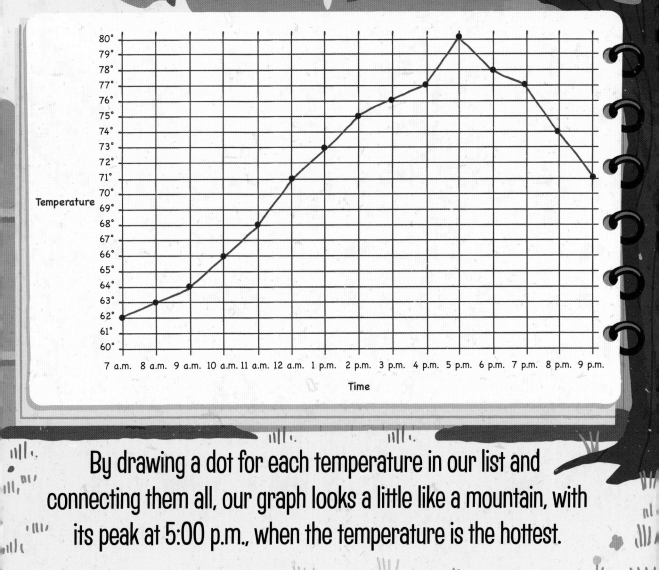

By drawing a dot for each temperature in our list and connecting them all, our graph looks a little like a mountain, with its peak at 5:00 p.m., when the temperature is the hottest.

GEOMETRY is about the size and shape of objects, like LINES, TRIANGLES, and CIRCLES.

We deal with geometry problems all the time.

At what ANGLE do I need to kick the soccer ball to get it in the corner of the goal?

It normally takes you **20 minutes** to walk **1 mile** to school each day. If you walked around your neighborhood for **60 minutes** at your normal speed, how far did you walk?

Using **ALGEBRA** we can write this question as an EQUATION using the numbers we know and a VARIABLE (X) for the number we *don't* know. Equations always include an EQUAL SIGN, meaning that what's on the left of the equal sign is the same as what's on the right.

Here's our question as an equation: $\dfrac{20 \text{ minutes}}{1 \text{ mile}} = \dfrac{60 \text{ minutes}}{X \text{ miles}}$

We SOLVE this equation to find out what value of X will make the two sides equal:

$$X \text{ miles} = \frac{60 \text{ minutes} \times 1 \text{ mile}}{20 \text{ minutes}}$$

Now we can use arithmetic on the right side of the equation: First, 60 times 1 is 60. Then, 60 divided by 20 equals 3. You walked 3 miles!

Numbers and math are part of almost everything we do. They help us describe and understand the world around us. So have fun with math!

GLOSSARY

ADDITION (uh-DISH-un): Combining two or more numbers together to get a total. $2+3=5$

ALGEBRA (AL-ju-bruh): A type of arithmetic that uses numbers and variables. $-2x+y=4$

ANGLE (ANG-gull): The difference between the direction of two lines that meet or intersect.

ARITHMETIC (uh-RITH-muh-tick): A type of mathematics dealing with the addition, subtraction, multiplication, and division

of numbers.

CIRCLE (SIR-cull): A closed shape made by a curved line whose ends meet. Every point on the circle is the same distance

from its center.

COUNTING: Adding things together to find a total. 🍎 + 🍎 + 🍎 = 3

DECIMAL (DESS-uh-mull): A number system that uses the ten numerals 0 through 9.

DIVISION (duh-VIH-zhun): Splitting one number into smaller equal parts; or calculating how many times one number is

contained within another number. $10 \div 2 = 5$

EQUAL SIGN (EEK-wool sine): A symbol (=) in an equation that means the numbers or variables on one side of it have the

same value as those on the other side. $10 - 6 = 4$

EQUATION (eek-WAY-zhun): Numbers, variables, or combinations of both placed on both sides of an equal sign, showing that

they are equal in value. $2 \times 3 = 6$

FRACTION (FRACK-shun): A number, such as $\frac{2}{3}$, that indicates the division of the number on top by the number on

the bottom.

GEOMETRY (jee-OM-uh-tree): A type of mathematics dealing with lines, angles, and shapes.

GRAPH (graff): A drawing that uses lines, shapes, and even colors to make a group of related numbers easier to understand.

LENGTH: A measure of how long something is, from one point to another.

LINE: A straight or curved length going from one point to another.

MATHEMATICS (MATH-uh-MAT-ix): The study of numbers, variables, and shapes, and the relationships between them.

MEASURE (MEH-zhur): A quantity that describes something about an object, like its length or weight.

MULTIPLICATION (mull-tuh-pluh-KAY-shun): Adding a number to itself a certain number of times. $3 \times 3 = 9$

NEGATIVE NUMBER: A number less than zero.

NUMBER LINE: A simple graph showing a group of numbers in order from small to large. $0\ 1\ 2\ 3\ 4\ 5$

NUMBER SYSTEM: A way of representing and organizing a set of numbers.

NUMERAL (NOOM-rull): A symbol used to represent a number. In the decimal number system, the numerals 0, 1, 2, 3, 4, 5, 6, 7, 8, and 9 are used.

POSITIVE NUMBER: A number more than zero.

SOLVE: Finding the correct answer to something, such as a mathematical equation.

SUBTRACTION (sub-TRACK-shun): Taking one number away from another to figure out the difference. $14 - 7 = 7$

TRIANGLE (TRY-ang-gull): A closed shape made of three lines. a c b

VARIABLE (VERY-uh-bull): A letter, such as "X," used in equations for a quantity we don't know the value of.

ZERO: A quantity equal to nothing. It's a number that's not positive or negative. $2 - 2 = 0$

Manufactured in Hong Kong in January 2018 by Toppan Printing

First Edition
22 21 20 19 18   5 4 3 2 1

Published by
Gibbs Smith
P.O. Box 667
Layton, Utah 84041

1.800.835.4993 orders
www.gibbs-smith.com

Designed by Greg Paprocki

Gibbs Smith books are printed on either recycled, 100% post-consumer waste, FSC-certified papers or on paper produced from sustainable PEFC-certified forest/controlled wood source. Learn more at www.pefc.org.

Library of Congress Control Number: 2017950749
ISBN: 978-1-4236-4936-6

Some important mathematicians . . .

Euclid (ca. 325–265 BCE)
Referred to as the father of modern geometry, his book *Elements* described the concepts of geometry for the first time in a clear and easy-to-understand manner. It also included information on number theory, factors, and prime numbers, and provided the basis of understanding for much of mathematics as late as the early twentieth century.

Isaac Newton (1643–1727)
He's best known for his theory of gravity, but also made important contributions to mechanics, optics, and chemistry. He invented a new branch of mathematics—calculus—to help him explain gravity. He explained the laws of motion, and also invented the reflecting telescope.

Ada Lovelace (1815–1852)
She developed the first computer algorithm, which was created for Charles Babbage's proposed computer known as the analytical engine. Beyond that, she was the first to recognize the potential of computers to be more than just calculating machines.

Emmy Noether (1882–1935)
One of the greatest mathematicians of the twentieth century, and considered by many to be the greatest woman mathematician ever, she made important contributions to abstract algebra and theoretical physics. Her way of thinking in fresh and original ways led to principles that unified algebra, geometry, linear algebra, topology, and logic.

Srinivasa Ramanujan (1887–1920)
With almost no formal mathematical training, he made important contributions to the fields of mathematical analysis, number theory, and infinite series. He was able to solve mathematical problems other mathematicians considered unsolvable.

Grace Hopper (1906–1992)
She was a computer programming pioneer who rose to the rank of US Navy rear admiral. She was one of the first programmers of the Harvard Mark I computer, and was later in charge of programming for the UNIVAC computer. She helped create the first computer language compiler, which led to the development of the popular COBOL programming language.

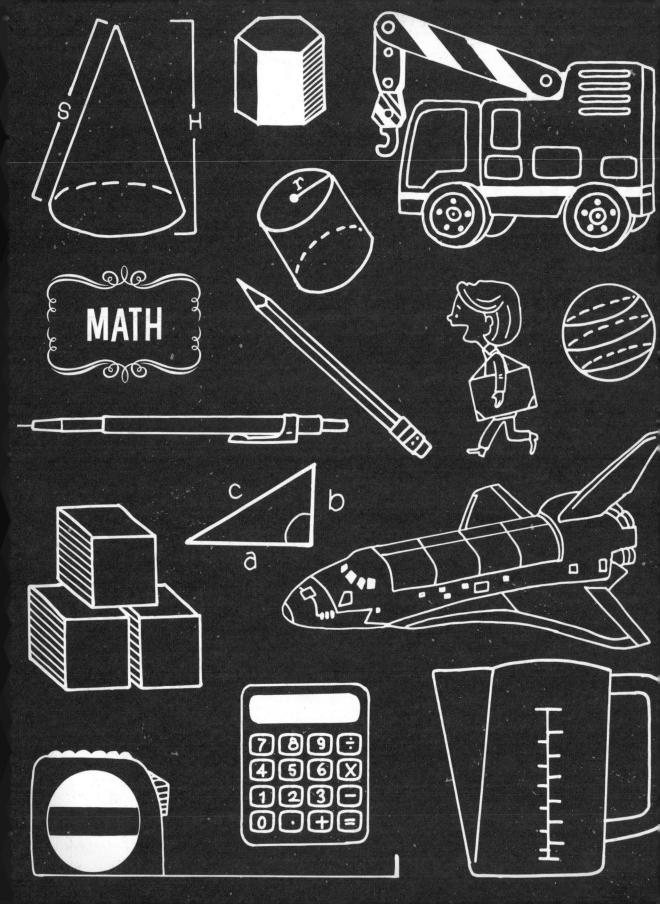